ENCHANTMENT

A COLLECTION OF POEMS

MASTER MARKOV

This collection, "Enchantment," is dedicated to those dreamers and darers who dance to the whispers of the inspiration of their own hearts.

May these verses resonate with the chords of your own journeys and serve you as a rational bridge to the madness of spirituality.

With gratitude,

Master Markov

Contents

Contents

Epigraph

"In the intertwining magic of existence, where nothing meets everything, and the mind whispers to the mighty soul, then in every beats of your heart-find Enchantment."

 - the whispering fairy

1. The Story of Andro

Childrens sitting by the fire, o the lovely, bright souls

Listen to an old story of my times, when I was too bold

In the world of magic and mystery, I played a humble role

It begins its mark when I travelled in time, to meet ancestors; old

I was sent back in time to an era of ancient days

To the land of legends and lores where wisdom lit the ways

I travelled by lightning, through the time's intricate maze

With an extraction mission I landed in a jungle ablazed.

Now, Inside the deep jungle, to a young elf I wished to speak.

She knew of Elixir Vitale along with many other things.

The difficulty: map's gone missing; and weather's all bleak.

Thus, I went into the tavern, under the mountain wings.

The bar sounds noisy, lots of fun there is.

I shall inquire here about the home of the elf supreme

Looked around I, to find a man seated wise.

He looked clean, savvy with the hair of a cream.

His name, I read Dr. Hermann Heuss, aye it is!

The person I talk to when assistance is in need.

Hello! Monsieur, its San Andro that speaks.

May I talk with you in private away from all this?

Welcome my friend! I am glad, but in disguise.

Hence, I shall see you a little later tonight.

"Sure doctor", nodded I, such unexpected his replies.

Taxed I was so accepted I, maybe the time is not right.

With a bleak smile he pointed to a room upstairs
I carried my bag and headed the stairways.
The bartender noticed and gave me quite a stare.
Avoided it and carried on with my unfruitful day.
I opened the door and found the room empty.
Checked myself in the mirror, my clothes were filthy.
Unpacked my bag and took the suit out.
And now I shall tell you what the journey is about.
I am a lone traveler in search of the pearl.
And to find it I must meet the elf girl.
Alone I have traveled with my traveler's pride.
I seek the wise one, who's riding the high tide.
I may look human but I'm a machine inside.
This dying vehicle is where my soul resides.
I hear the elf is magic, yet unknown her whereabouts.
Now it's up to me to figure it all out.
Created I was through my dad from cogs and springs.
I wasn't born by reproduction of biological things.
He, my dad named me Andro, an anomalous humanly being.
And assured me I will be a ruler of all men; I will be a king.
But the sad story is he died in the process, of old age.
Unable complete me, hindered by the time constraint,
I therby remain, devoid of age and emotions like rage.
However, he left a guiding letter to his son, a saint.
The letter stated to find the elf, who dwelled in the mountain.
Some instructions about finding the pearl, for a perpetual fuel.
All to live an immortal life, to guide men to an elevated point.
This pearl could power me for eternity, with the energy of Exa-joule.
Yet I am a child though, not more than some 13 years old.

I am to be a vanguard of a movement, that's what I was told.
Sometimes, I doubt how am I to lead anyone with my faulty parts.
I am just a machine and lack emotions of humanly hearts.
Too much of my backstory, too much into thoughts
Yeah, I know, quite tragically I am some mental-naut.
Wait but… I do feel pity for I self-loathe me a lot.
I doubt myself too, although to do so I wasn't taught.
"Forget this! forget that!", just detach from this n' that.
I must quickly focus in the present, for a task I have got.
A glance out of the window revealed a black wildcat.
With resolve, I decided to move into night as a ready robot.
I made the bed ready and put my head down.
Heard a knock on the door, wondered who was around.
I opened the door and saw the bartender with a bottle of whiskey.
I invited her in, and the lady seemed all frisky.
I asked her why she came at this late hour.
She said she wanted to sweeten my mood which was sour.
I thought of it as a chance to know more about the place.
And her interest in me seemed clear by her gaze.
She opened the bottle and filled our glasses.
Suddenly I teleported in the matter of flashes.
I can see us talking but I'm not in the room.
I feel like a wizard rising amidst the brume.
Hours passed since I flashed out, disordered, and fell asleep.
What was in the bottle?, that took me on such trip.
Surreal memories were planted in my head.
Of when I spoke to the elf and knew where the pearl was made.
Awoke I the next day, in the room on my bed.
I don't know when I came back and when I got laid.

Still with the tangible memory of nothing that happened.
Words uttered from my mouth, but my speech was slackened.
I asked the bartender what she had poured me, as she awoke.
She laughed this time as if I told her a good joke.
Then she told me the doctor is waiting on the second floor
I bathed in hot water and dressed, therefore.
Hurriedly I went upstairs and met him there.
Today he dropped disguise like he forgot his fear.
Now I told him why I was here, visiting this land.
But when I asked him directions, he tells me where I stand.
Then I took few gold shillings out, felt a fee was implied.
He grinned his teeth out and my queries finally he replied.
Wishing me good luck for my journey ahead
He suggested me, to go find and meet the redhead.
I asked him next question, wondering where I should go now.
To find the redhead but where? And how?
He looked at nearby church and said he doesn't know.
And asked me to pray to the lord and then go with the flow.
I packed my bag hurriedly and set in motion.
The jolly bartender offered me now two magic potions.
I asked her, will it knock me out like the last brew, she gave?
She said its magic elixir, don't be a fool and be brave.
Yes! that made quite a sense for to focus the task at hand.
I must become a brave lad, who can even stand the hottest sand.
Well! I have some objectives now, to go to the nearby church.
And I need to meet this redhead, wherever she has perched.
I asked the bartender which way the church is.
She says two minutes into the jungle, an old building there is.
Just follow the narrow pavement and don't knock on the door.

Also, she mentioned not to touch the candles or walk on the floor.
O! Lord, what does that mean? Not to walk on the floor
I mean, I understand not knocking but not walking? What for?
Finally, I reached the church, it was colossal but dark outside.
I wondered in which chamber does the redhead reside.
So, I did roam around the building, tip-tap-tiptoe.
I saw one room on the first floor, with a particular glow.
Well, the plan was simple now just climb to that floor.
Sneak into the room without even opening the door.
So, I did that I used my android strength to climb.
I entered through the lunette and touched the window chime.
Then I see the redhead alone suffering in her torment
She was sleeping before but now woke up, because of my scent.
The story of redhead was she was delirious in her death bed.
Interrupt me none, I'm conversing with gods she said.
Kept muttering no sense as if she was all coherent and clear.
What help could she be of, she seems half mad already, o dear?
Footsteps I heard outside the corridor, so I hid myself in the cupboard.
O' and inside that large cupboard, there were items that appeared old.
I became fascinated, as amidst those craps, I found a big shiny sword.
I just stole the blade, it was sharp, in addition had a grip of a gold.
I heard the members; they were talking about tying up the redhead.
They were inclined to sedate her, forever so, she will remain insane.
Brought ropes, holy water, and a cross to make a show of exorcism.
Typical show of humans where they practise self sabotaging schism.
The redhead was tortured to the very end of her resistance.
They left her alone to rot, which I saw as a possible chance.
Emerged from the shadows, not in the way you might expect.
This lady was in state of comatose, yet life, her eyes did reflect

Then an idea struck into my head, to feed the lady the magic potion.
She drank it on my request, and it calmed down her rising emotion.
In jolly mood she tells me how happy she is for the drink of vial
Gladly, she tells me the pearl can be found in the Stopplmoult aisle.
The journey to the Stopplmoult was hard as tis was away.
Since I began my mission, I couldn't stop the midway.
Alone I hiked and made the climb to the Stopplmoult top.
Then, I saw it in the top of tower, the pearl kept spot.
I went near the spot to pick the pearl up.
The elf appears out of nowhere and tells me to stop.
I tell her I have made this hard journey just for the pearl.
Now, she tells me I can't have it, petty this elf girl.
The elf frustrated, points me with her staff.
Then yells if I touch the pearl, she will slice me in half.
I bow down to her and ask her to spare my life.
And tell her I am not a man but a machine, a device.
She calmed down and showed me mercy, in her good grace.
Tells me she was waiting for me and puts smile on her face.
I tell her I was invented by a man who died before I was completed.
I operate by fuel and need the pearl before it is depleted.
She says she feels sorry about my dying situation.
And asks me to do her one task, in good association.
I tell her I am willing to do what she wants.
As long as for my service, the pearl that she grants.
Now she tells me the task is to: catch a mocking jay.
She lured it many times but each time it flew away.
The task is hefty, to catch such a smart bird.
As the bird is special, it utters human words.
Now with no knowledge about its exact location

I set forth my tracking with a little information.
I was told it will be roaming free in the valley of veil.
Despite making an arduous attempt what if I fail?
I went to the valley of veil, everyone appeared as saint.
They spoke in foreign tongue, quite hard to decode.
But I am a machine and I see the wall through its paint.
Wquipped with features of the future, some unnatural modes.
I won't reveal them all, but I do have certain brainpower.
Which I call the gift of my creator, my nurturer, my lord.
Stopping the time for a certain interval, is my superpower.
But when I practice this, I lose pulses of life, which I can't afford.
Apparently, this valley was haunted, ghost roamed here midnight.
Heard it from these people who were chatting about it every time.
I wanted to meet this demonic spirit, to know about its plight.
And maybe exercise my power, to devour this sorry slime.
My next move I planned, to wander the streets at night.
So, I may encounter this ghost terrorizing the public, grave-time.
Well! Yeah, I caught the glimpse of this ghost looking for a fight.
I couldnt hold my laughter when I saw a village monk burning thyme.
I followed the ghost slowly to its hiding place, a dark cave.
It wasn't a hungry devil but some compelled weak slave.
How? You may ask as you don't know what I saw there.
There was a puppet master, the town-chief spreading fear.
The chief was compelling people to hide during the night.
So, he may proceed with his plan in plain sight without a care.
He was robbing houses, to amass a wealth tight.
Deceiving the innocent masses to claim a higher chair.
Now I had two choices to fulfill my personal mission.
Or I could help the pupil by lifting chief's veil of power.

I chose the latter, for I could spare some time in this position.
If I did nothing then this ghost can spread like wildflower
The plan was simple, just trap both ghost and its master.
So, people will be aware of the horror and start a new chapter.
Gladly, I stopped time for an hour and put grills at the gate.
Few days later the townsfolks found out whom to hate.
Now to catch the mocking jay, I needed some assistance.
I found out a psychic who was living temporarily in the town.
I went inside her tent and told I am a man from land of distant.
She pulled out a deck of cards, from her long and bright gown.
She asks me o good lad, what do you want to know?
I told her, you are a psychic. Why not just give me a good show?
A smirk she did give me and told me you will soon see the snow.
You will get what you desire, and it will end all your woes.
Okay! Quite convincing, yet non sensical somewhat
Felt my pocket and took some gold shillings out of that.
Then she holds my hand and requests me to provide the potion
I was hesitant with her behest since it was pure manipulation.
But before the trade, I did inquire why she asks for the potion.
I was baffled by her request, her unnatural sought, of emotion.
She was hesitant to express, her wishes in the beginning.
Until I provoked her to a state, she went into a spinning.
Then she explained her plight, says she needs it to survive.
I inquired again what energy from such chemicals she derives.
Acting looney, she was unwilling to come up to me direct.
Constant lies about her own life; through her mouth I detect.
Being compelled I stopped the time right away in anger.
I do an inspection of the tent heeding every nook and corner.
To my shock I find fascinating objects in her bag

She had multiple potions and costumes, the maniac hag
To my surprise she was the same - bartender and the redhead
Acting psychic now whom I pitied, as a deliriant in her deathbed.
Then those visions of having spoken to the elf, rings a loud bell.
It seems it is a long game, this woman could also be the elf, as well.
Didn't wish to waste more minutes so just went back to my stool.
Yup certainly the elf girl is magic, so to play wise I must act as a fool.
I let her have her ways with her demands of that potion.
Possessing it for any false power mustn't be the object of my notion.
Finally, I re-account that the reason for all my personal woes,
Is my desire to intervene in, which only accumulates the foes.
Yet I do trust my dad and he certainly didn't mean to harm.
The pearl I must chase, outplaying over the elf and her charm.
This object I seek, the pearl is some powerful and rare artifact.
I know they are formed under depth of seas, with locations inexact.
I question how it's different from the other pearls that form.
By changing my own mechanism, I wonder how I may reform.
I could exercise my time stopping power, to seize the pearl.
But without the elf isn't around, I cannot risk such a swindle.
Instead, by catching the mocking-jay, I'll meet the girl,
I might deceive her this time, a certain instinct starts to kindle
I planned a clever trap, meticulously staged.
I built a great garden, with an intention to have the bird caged.
I waited for it to show up many days and night.
And it came around seeking shelter one day, after sunlight.
The bird was finally caught in the trap that I laid.
Caught by surprise it asked for help, becoming afraid.
I found pity in its condition, but free I couldn't let it go.
I caught it to give to the elf, that much it did know.

The bird then asks me, "I am to be traded in what return?"
I tell it I need the pearl from the elf if that is your concern.
The bird says I am stupid, for the elf is not to be trusted.
She will never give away the precious pearl, it was to be deducted.
What options did I have? I couldn't trust the bird as well.
But the elf is deceitful, to that it rings a certain loud bell.
The bird then goes on saying, the pearl I can help you to get.
When the elf asks me to shoot it, shoot the cunning elf instead.
I travelled to the Stopplmoult aisle, after the sunrise.
When I showed up there, she was ready for the sacrifice.
She put a gun in my hands, it was fully loaded.
I was planning to shoot her there; it was not decoded.
She tells me to shoot the bird, once she finishes her ritual.
Then she chants certain mantras in a fashion that was unusual
At sharp noon she finishes her exceedingly long chants
She raises the cage mid-air and my shooting she demands.
It all happened so fast; I was confused the whole while.
This demonic elf from her actions, looks like an agoraphile.
With a gun fully loaded, I am the man in power.
Yet with any exercise of this, my world will be sour.
In my dilemma, I don't go for the shooting.
The thought of shooting anybody was very polluting.
So, I shoot the gun emptying all bullets, in the open air.
The gun was loaded with blanks, of which I became aware.
The elf laughs aloud, and she tells me I did the best.
To see that how I would act, was the elf's test.
Then she proudly presents the pearl to me
And her companion the bird she lets go free.
I take a deep breath in satisfaction; glad it was just a test.

And my happy moment starts you can comprehend the rest.
Its paramount that one respects every surrounding life.
If one understands that it should cause no social strife.
Now for the final integration, I attach the pearl into my part.
I feel an ecstatic pump, that comes through a throbbing heart.
It feels surreal, since it made me now complete as a man.
Hence, the next task begins, the next part of my creator's plan
I have to travel back to the origin where present starts
From here the journey began, and back there I chart
where my coin will be tossed, head or tail of dime
Embark I shall on the next mission, through space and time.

2. Descendants of Nova

The descendants of Nova
Casted down to the ground
None have remembered, to take a look around
Stitched with serious sorrows
Condemned with deceits and lies
They don't know the tomorrow
Bounded with the endless ties
They fall again into the pattern
And keep worsening theirs days
Ask repeatedly for a godly lantern
When with their own spirit, could light their ways
All things take time to fluorish, to gather, to shine and grow
I keep asking they develop faith, and just go with the flow.

3. Caged parrot

What songs would the songbird sing?
And for whom? How will they ever fly?
They have never given it any try
Their soul remains soaked but still its dry
They've lived tamed in the cages
With meals, brought down in plates
Feathers, they had, were never all shed
They don't dream to fly in their silver bed
They hear the moth's flutter
Yet they haven't heard it true
In pain they always utter
Since life must be endured through

4. Searching for the roots

I have trodden fairer lands with my dirty boots
I have explored the muddy parts in search of my roots
And I concluded it many times
I am like indivisible mathematical primes
I am the root of myself, a strange number
And there's no other like me, such bummer
Yet I can't stop to expect
Doubting creator's neglect
I must be a half of a whole
Since there's parity even in magnetic pole
Shouldn't there be someone to complete me?
Augmented remain I, with no one to deplete me?
For what should I then pray?
I am a cup without a tray
Alone I rejoice and I mourn
Why was I even born?

5. Her beauty

Her beauty is of a sweet bird's song
Indescribable by human tongue
She can cast spells to any man
Her walk is like an angel's dance
Her skin is of splendid white
The reflection of her is divine light
Creator perfectly placed her bone
In my closed eyes, I see her in monochrome
Her speech is dazzlingly artistic
Pondering on her, I have become a mystic
Who says the fairy is an imagination?
Made from a mind's construction
I have seen one in this life time
Deduction I now make in rhymes

6. The adamant monsoon

The summer was sold to golden lies
The monsoon came so I opened my eyes
When I looked up and gazed the sky
I saw two massive clouds hovering by
One white, soft and agile
Another dark and in deep slumber
Yet none rained, cause the summer was sold
They hated one another as both felt miserable and old
And though both longed to meet
Their metamorphosis wouldn't let them exist
One filled with beauty and another a beast
And it didn't rain south, north, west or east
However, a final collision of time
Was inevitable, cuz what they did was a crime
To invite the joyful autumn again
Yes, there has to be one refreshing rain
They both levitated higher to roar and thunder
Then demolished the evil pirate's plunder
Now since they both lost their coldness
Were born anew despite their oldness
They look so happy entangled around
At the end they both fell and rained abound.

7. In the lonely nights

Dusk brings out the darkness's embrace
With the death of sun's face
Lonesome nights where I ponder alone
About the future and the days bygone
No companion to share this time with
just the distant memories I had bequeath
looking up and seeing thousands of stars
brings my mind to my very own scars
I slip back to the closed chambers of heart
Then there I remain engaged in my art
Aesthetic, amazing, abstracts of my mind
Illuminating visions and thoughts refined
Who knows what doors these creations come?
Enchantment, disbelief and freedom's sum

8. To the Temptress

You knew I lived in imagination
So, you dragged me to the ground
I knew you roamed in dreamy nation
When I felt you standing around
Woman of the century, you: heartbreaker
Like weapon of the future, you: lightsaber
You: unapologetic temptress
A concubine free of stress
Conjurer of false bliss
Heard you offer stranger your lips
You are the nightmare's scream
Falsifier of my gifted dreams
The unnerving wind of the wild
Wish you were the mother to my child
And who gave you the right to walk away?
From the man who wanted your night and day
I know I never asked you to stay
And I grow awry with guilt every day.

9. Your Wondrous kind

You got what you wanted treading my mind
I lost what I chanted day in and day out
I got my vision, and it turned me blind
Now I see the world and what people are about
I praised you in proses and got hated instead
I learnt my lesson, through love I assayed
Now I call you the monster, a marvelous devil
And you call me a liar and the notorious rebel
Is that the consolation prize you give to all who admires you?
And do you show hell to everybody who desires you?
I attempted to show you what I mined
You rejected them all and hated my grind
Questions in hundreds are gathered on my mind
I don't want your beauty and your wonderous kind

10. Piece of my heart

Peace is in solitude away from you
And life is in memories given by you
My breath stops and I fall into insanity
And my heart aches alone in this tragedy
Lucky are lovers who have found each other
And lost are souls who never meet their another
Your image is hard to retain within my heart
Cuz with it, Happiness ends and my crying starts
My life is now a pity and my smile is lost
My hopes are drowned and my feelings tossed
I wish you could accept my apology
I wish you could end this animosity
Waited I have many days repeating your name
To live with you till death is now my only aim
Forgetting you is harder with each passing year
And cared you have none for this love, o dear
Devasted, I have become and sorrows repeats
Your presence is desired with every passing beat
Why are you so hard to love? And why am I so desperate?
Why does your forgotten image repeatedly generate

11. Should parallel lines meet at infinity?

The forward movement that matters
Is a Vector pointing towards the novelty factor
The object supposed at the end of the times
Is not a song or poem that rhymes
Unshifting polarity is the cause of crime
Beg all you wish, no one will spare a dime
Don't trap yourself, take that liberty
Invest in yourself or suffer poverty
Don't consume, don't submit, don't follow
Condense the knowledge or forever remain hollow
Emabark on the journey towards the self discovery
Make the time to achieve good feats in summary
Although the source is distant from the sink
A certain forces always favor the link
Even the lines which are parallel, do meet at infinity
Leave the calculations asides and trust the affinity.

12. My strangest dream

Time, with its great power
transforms nature as above so below
where dreams grow like flower
and disintegrate like melting snow

So, I keep on searching
for something, that's eternally mine
a thought, keeps suggesting
to chase for the light of the divine

To elaborate with rhymes
It's not a story
To be eradicated by time
It's not a transient glory

It's the loudest scream
which guides, every steps I take
My strangest dream
A majestic mountain, beside a loneliest lake

It's a sacred fire
Imbued with constant longing.
My ultimate desire
For a transcendental bonding.

I aspire, to reach for infinity
To become, one with the source.
But this wishful affinity
Seems unattainable by humanly force.

Yet, I carry a dream
To be cognizant of the creator's plan
To know the supreme
And rise above, as a man

I know, infinity is far
thus the journey will be long
But I am aiming for stars
And I have to be strong

Steps I have taken
Albeit, small and few
hoping, one day to awaken
and witness a clearer view

of the creator's magnificence
filled with perfection
Under whose munificence
I desire my own - resurrection

13. The two variables of existence

The two variables of existence
Like two parts of a sentence
Made in the heaven
Half of the eleven
Sound of innocence
opposite of nonsense
purpose of existence
survival for presence
quarrel of the opposite
death won't suppose it
mountain by the lake
attacks on the fake
bent to the ground
won't make a sound
like wind blows the dust
remains unmotivated by lust
longing for a mix
cuz there isn't another fix
does it ring a bell?
No. you won't get what I tell.

14. The fool of tarot

The fool is a wanderer
the hateful squanderer
he stands on a precipice
as if, he is about to jump off a cliff
His life has no benefit
and he avoids reading any glyph
he has everything he needs
reflected it is: in his deeds
he is the innocent
with dreams that are dissonant
He is the anointed harbinger
ignorant; he is as an arbiter
A faithful dog follows him
he keeps singing godly hymns
he is like those happy lad
spreading joy makes him glad

15. Unclaimed boon

Touched was I by snow
Yet I denied, when I had to bow
Consequences heavy I endured
And lost was all what I adored
My pride was turned into dust
My bubble had abrubtly burst
I fell hard and I fell deep
Into the vortex of hardship
Broken was my trust in God
Like some foliage which a tree forgot
I sank into the continual depth
Stolen were all the possessions I kept
And although I abhored the living
I continued forgiving and praying
Nothing brought me a hint of joy
I existed but as a puppet, a toy

16. House of cards

I used to fabricate dreams the whole night
But in my heart, I knew something wasn't right
Soon the reality brought wind, storm and rain
And in the same way that footprint vanish in vain
My house of cards was also swept away
Each night little by little, into the storm, slowly
Clue, I had in my mind was an empty: none
The clouds on which my castle rested, was gone
I ponder on it, why it had to happen: the reality
I was doing fine with my distorted rationality
I hope there is a bigger force in a bigger picture
Which caused this turmoil: an unwanted mixture
Of rain, wind and my delicate house of cards
I still carry inside my heart its deadly shards
It wasn't just a dream that was swept away
It's the scars that came back into life to stay

17. Corpse's song

Goodbye!
To your prolific days, I bid farewell
To an eternal doom, I invite you in
You had so much when you were born
Now the ropes of wishes has been torn
I am sure you have heard me before
Calling you from the closed door
But now we meet in this conjunction
Abandoned you have your life's compulsion
Hello!
I am your corpse the stationary kind
You, the forfeiter of visions, became a blind
Trapped is your body like sands in the shore
Its awful smell all mankind abhor
Gathered you have many foes and faults
Locked are your aspirations in some deep vaults
They now say, you were gone to soon
I wish for your life if God granted a boon

18. A standing tree

A man cannot change what he sees
What he sees, decides what he feels
What he feels, decides what he does
Its the law of nature thats how it goes
But what he can see is through a reflection of himself
His judgement and his own preconceived notions
what he sees is actually himself
His inner ideas, and his own concoctions
What if? He truly chooses... not to see
Just like one tall standing tree
Growing alone even in the wild
unwary that one day its wood will be filed
By this, will he be free?
Or is it what he ought to be?
Just living to breathe and to grow
unbothered by its predators that roam below

19. Torrent of Flabbergast

The fire set off the life
It lent its spark to chaos unclean
which became the one, unwilling to oblige
How could it? it hadn't an idea of divine

It is the chaos unclean, but it never forgot
Indeed it could feel in it deep
but with memory none of what it lost
Except in silent scream of dream

"let thy torch go and let my fire light
I knew the way perhaps I could lead
To the land of the primordial self
which speaks the language rich"

One day it spoke in voices loud
In ears of someone, who lost his I
he heard, he noticed, it was profound
tales it were, of time immemorial, tales of the I

it was insanity, this fits of madness
it was a touch of unseen and vision of unheard
torrent of flabbergast, known but strange
In songs, in mystery and in stories. In freedom.

20. Shat-Chit-Anand

I sharpened myself, a fine crystal
wishing to contain your light
But! god you abode, in the unreachable astral
to where, no man I know, made the flight
Everywhere I see sins and sadness
Have all my angels fled?
despaired and discontent with madness
Are these all I'm now left to be?
In the stances of my trance
I get to feel you, so rare
Just a glimpse, and rest is the demon's dance
tell me o holy? Do you even care?
"Lie" it spoke, think again
"Did I abandon you or did you?"
you warp yourself, in a blanket
and wait for the touch of dew?
Did you ever seek the Allah?
was it the whole, you wished?
you lived like a man, with personal plans
caring none of the divine, you sleep
I'm awake, I've recalled my unspoken vows
today's night, where all my grasp must die
wishes, hatred swept away now
I realize my ego, and the life of lie

"Oh you dear, I spoke to you clear
few hours a day in all four seasons
and you repelled me dear, with irrational fear
of constricting conditions, the only prison"
"Yet I am for you, and can't be away
As you are the pottery and me the clay"
know it being "to worship yourself
is to worship the god, himself"
Now come to me dear, and join the ride
Remember our home, that heavenly place?
meet me there, and I shall embrace you again,
where it's the end of all reasons, the holy space

21. Merry Songs

All merry songs turn sad
They lose their tune with the tide of time
like rosy lips crumble before winter
The lyrics then are replaced
by better and smoother rhymes.
Only the music is taken
to be sung by another one
With new and fewer lines.
Recorded again, by instruments
of another time
And so shall it be known,
the music is the rhyme
which transcends the eternal time
which hold the cup of the divine
That how the world works in its design.

22. Eschatology

History is a shockwave of eschatological process
Hidden remains the pain in the spirit of prowess
A mirror traveling backwards at the speed of light
Think of it as a dog that won't bark but bite
To reach the object at the end of the time
The terror must submit before the thoughts sublime
Uncountable flaws and hopes they exist
But the desire to surpass all, one cannot resist
It over-shines the brightest and gets pulled with strength
Explore its deepest depth and stretch to a longer length
Keep the negations at its bays
As nights follows every hectic days
Light the fire and let the smoke out
Elevated you are, if you figure what it's about...

23. Art of war

It's one thing to wield a weapon but another to kill
It one thing to destroy the Lanka and another to become evil
The rivers, thousands of years have changed their flow
And thickest of the tree has become hollow
Knowest it all but on the branch the owl perches
Awaits patiently and when time, the leopard lurches
Dance to the beat even If you're sick with sorrow
If today's not your time, you know there is tomorrow
Mind your own business don't draw the first blood
If you know you must, then swim towards the flood
Attention, Attention!! it's now your time to rise
Show them you don't care and attack by surprise

24. History the mystery

History is a mystery
Of universal tapestry
Meteors has claimed the dinosaur
And trapped, in labyrinth hungry minotaur
Future hates the past
Probing rockets never blast
God can guide ships without masts
And us human believe we shall last
With our erroneous definitions of life,
Repeated remains the social strife
Amok are the criminals, despite
Deadly commission of crimes
Someone must pass them sentence
And compel, the culprit for repentance

25. About chasing light

Don't compel me to admire the lesser light
Don't compel me to take part in your fight
I have battles of my own
Let me sing in my own tone
There are bigger demons I wish to slay
Your mundane games I won't play
How about you find your own reason?
In the appropriate season
Then you might be strong enough to see
A stronger cause, an answer to be
No, I'm not telling you to forsake your world
But don't make this miner pay for the gold.

26. King of the jungle

I yearn to be that which can't be destroyed
To become like a lion that cannot be annoyed
Something to hold onto in this transient space
A permanent bliss that can't be displaced
Yet the time is a tide with its ebb and flow
And changes the nature, as above so below
Every longing disperses like melting snow
And gives the seeker a deadly blow
Truth be told, nothing should matter
To a lion that is the threatener, an attacker
But the technology from this evil earth
Has killed lions that were the king by birth
It's the flies and fleas that rules the forest
And irritates our kings and queens the dearest
Hidden in day and haunting at night
Engulfing the nature staying out of sight
Tormenting the host where they reside
Making the lion realize its faulty pride

27. Mightiest of All

The sweetness of the moon
The curve of a spoon
Delightful rainy night
A bird's first flight

Comes down to one fun fact
It's all the almighty's act
Behind the screen running a show
And helping us out in this earth below

But one thing rumbles loud inside
Right and wrong how can one decide?
Maybe there is a theory
Of this spectacular story

And maybe a guide as well
O lord! that would be swell
But if you bring faith in your existence
Only may you overcome the resistance

Mark the wisdom of these words
Neither pen is mighty nor a sword
The mighiest is the persistent spirit
In his efforts who remains empiric

28. Mankind no longer stranded

The aliens have landed
Hip-hip, Ho!
Mankind no longer stranded
Hip-hip, Ho!!
They say it took them forever
To diagnose our unhealthy fever
Now they have landed in the sand
We will welcome them with our band
We will provide them an earthly home
Gather all the nymphs and the gnomes
They have travelled from distant galaxy
To further their gifts and legacy
Praises to the almighty lord
Unpassable streams we shall ford
Then settle ourselves in space
Blessings to their hallowed race

29. Cycle of new beginning

It's the cycle of new beginning
The age to create a happy ending
The bombs have plain-ed the territory
Time to sow saplings of our new story
Skies have cleared since the storm
Angels have fallen on earth to reform
Days are as always, limited in number
Awaited we were in the antechamber
Let's spread our wings and leap to fly
Soar high in whatever nature supply
And teach our youngers to do the same
With a little faith, they have in god's name
The journey up hill was taxing but the view: breathtaking
Dancing we are to do, on the plateau will be elating
We'll love, we'll play in our lofty tunes
The consecration of human soul will resume

30. Rise of the mortal man

Sunken into the sea the bottles of hopes
Torn are now the tethered ropes
The plight of eternity was never answered
And the fight has ended among the monster
The mortal man has risen
He has abandoned his sorrows
Now he has taken the matters in hands
Oozes out power from his DNA strands
He has no false hope or truthful fears
Neither he will shed for any, his precious tears
Love's his motto and life, is his hope
He has summited mountain and will now slide down the slope

31. Man's exploration

When the man began to explore
Smelt gold, iron from the ores
Filled remained his treasure stores
Soon his stories became mere folklore
Then the man ended his "explore"
Inquired the legends and the folklore
Harvest filled his store
His house was made multi-floored
Time passed and he became awry
He noticed his strives to be sorry
So, he realized he lost what he bore
As he searched for richness acquiring ores
But time and then, a wave seep through
From the walls of ego as he sleeps
Does he remember that he forgot?
Nay. He just forgot he remembers.

32. God's intent

The vast of nature sweetly baffles me
The beauty has been seized yet beguiling
What must be the god's intent?
What is the destiny impending?
Is it in the worship of Gopalas?
Or in the carnage of Kurukshetra?
Perhaps it's in the sleep of Vishnu?
Or in the rejoicing of Shiva?
Then a faith dawn onto me
That he is the one in all
He, who is shining in the shade
And making noise in silence
I know it and feel it somewhere
That transcendent is out there
Pulling me with eternal desire
With the divinity I wish to aspire

33. My Land

My land is an imaginary one
Where the sun shines when it's cold
And the moon cools down the heat
It has magic aroma in its air
Where every blooming flower,
Has freshness of the supreme
It has truth in its happiness
And meaning in it bliss
However, far may I look
I see rooted in it... deep, the glory
Just like one in a beautiful story
Where sorrows just freeze and cease
where I exists one with the holy
My joys makes sense truly
Where, the love is made the purpose
And eternal harmony exists

34. Our tale

My love,
Forever seems shorter, to live a life with you
And all dreams can shatter, to put you in my view
Heart, I had one, now its dissected in two
They beat in pair and stops to remember just you
matters it none what or who I am
Fluid my emotions are now a jam
Peek into my soul, through your eyes
leave the gossips that tells you the lies
We were made in heaven as a pair
It's not just words it's an axiom, my dear
embrace me tight and cherish me in your heart
love me like I do to you, and our tale shall start

35. The Supreme Truth

Rest he shall in the night and seize his days
When He will know what he knew always

Obtained will be the answers crystal clear
Of two questions: who he is and why is he here?

With ignorance of faulty decision people fall
Know that supreme truth is the sum of it all

He who forever, in himself, puts his trust
wont travel by the path that's dangerously short

One who remains brave and declares the joy
pleasures in peace, opening gate to god's ploy

36. Go win it all

Sometimes wishes do come true
Amidst obstacles, when you break through
Somedays, your heart rises
In a whirlpool of infinite prizes
But somedays you are down
In your face appears a heavy frown
Tear drops will fall from your sore eyes
From loved ones you depart with goodbyes
And dead gone are those merriment
Trapped you are like rats in experiment
In the void of distasteful experience
Tightly bounded in the highest fence
But no don't accept this defeat
Rise and shine with extraordinary feat
Go prove all the haters wrong
Be bold and be spectacularly strong
Your time will come to live your dreams
Don't listen to the noises of negative screams
Faster and farther, you can jump
Your wish is the truth which should trump
Go roar like thunder and have a ball
Because today's the day to win it all

37. Around Her

Around her, The noisy trumpets of heart, rings louder
Probably the spells of her perfumes and powders
The surfaces of my soul and mind become a warzone
Similar to the depletion by UV of the atmospheric ozone
The circuitry of my neural network goes haywire
The pages of my precious books are set on fire
Through her eyes I see my own reflection
And amidst her I experience total affection
I talk with her everyday in my imagination
But around her, compelled I am to take no action
I know she expects some reactions
But I practice - cautious precautions
Just so we never divide into fractions
And I keep experiencing the attractions
Helpless, I am when my senses point at your angle
How was I to know? I would be forever entangled
Yet I wish to collide with this vampire
But to look back she has no desire
Eternally till eternity, cordially and carefully
As always yours dearly and sincerely,
Your one true admirer, quite clearly.